10

12

14

C000278147

21

22

25

27

29

Images, unless stated, are
copyright States of Guernsey

Illustrations by Brian Byron

GUERNSEY HISTORY
TIMELINE

includes an illustrated
timeline telling the history
of Guernsey and its people

PAGE
34-35

HROUGHOUT THIS GUIDE REFERENCES ARE MADE TO
MPORTANT PARTS OF THE CASTLE. A MAP ON PAGE
4 - 35 WILL HELP YOU FIND THE SURVIVING FEATURES.

# Introduction
## the story begins

Castle Cornet, Guernsey's great fortress, stands on a rock outside the busy harbour of St Peter Port. A stronghold of the English Crown for nearly 800 years, it has a special place in the story of Guernsey.

Guernsey is the second largest of the Channel Islands. Separated from the landmass of Europe at the end of the Ice Age as sea levels rose, a natural harbour developed on the east coast and it is this which defines much of its history. Archaeological studies suggest that human activity on the island dates from around 7000 BC.

The Island's communities appear to have thrived; possibly because of their advantageous position on the sea trade route between what is now France and England. During the Roman period (50 BC - AD 400), St Peter Port was a busy Roman town. Later, it became part of the Norman Empire - embracing the French culture. However, in 1204 when King John lost Normandy to France, the Channel Islands, though constitutionally independent, remained under the English Crown. Guernsey's harbour became strategically important and Castle Cornet was built to protect it.

GUERNSEY HISTORY
TIMELINE  7000BC  5000BC  3000BC  100

7000BC-1250

Channel Islands separated from Europe as sea levels rose at end of Ice Age

A natural harbour develops on the east coast of Guernsey

Island communities appear to have thrived

During th Roman peric St Peter Po was a bus tow

4

# Medieval Castle
## building the walls

The islet on which the castle stands was accessible by foot at extreme low tides. It is one of a number of rocks which form a protective boundary to the harbour of St Peter Port.

Construction on the original fortification probably began around 1250. The entrance to the medieval castle was reached along a low, rocky path on the islet and through a gate-house on its north-eastern side. The outer walls of the castle, which occupied the upper levels of the rock, enclosed several buildings.

These included a chapel, a half round tower or bastion to the west, and a square tower, the Tour Carré to the south.

Further walls were built later to enclose a shelf of land below the cliff to the north, as well as a lower gate. This gate had a ditch and drawbridge and was still approached from the east. The walls supported a walkway which would have greatly aided the defence of those inside.

*The site of the castle during the Roman period* 1
*Building the first castle* 2
*The medieval castle, circa 1450* 3

2  3

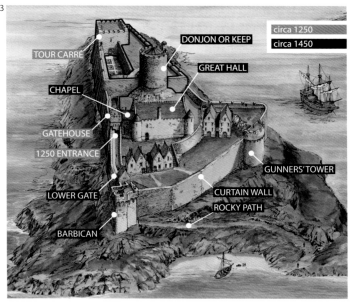

TOUR CARRÉ

DONJON OR KEEP

GREAT HALL

CHAPEL

circa 1250
circa 1450

GATEHOUSE

1250 ENTRANCE

GUNNERS' TOWER

LOWER GATE

CURTAIN WALL

ROCKY PATH

BARBICAN

1204

King John loses Normandy to France. Channel Islands though constitutionally independent, remain under English Crown

1250

Castle Cornet built to defend Guernsey's harbour

# The French Threat
## the early history

The early history of the castle is dominated by the continuing threat from France.

In 1337 the King wrote to the Bailiffs and Jurats of Guernsey & Jersey and to the Warden, Thomas de Ferrers, ordering them *'to cause the castles of La Cornet and Gurry* (Gorey Castle, Jersey) *to be provided with men-at-arms and other infantry, armour and victuals, as the king had learned that they were in great danger for lack of such provision.'*

As the French swept through the Channel, Jersey and Guernsey were attacked and in September 1338, Castle Cornet was taken. The French held the castle for a total of seven years despite several attempts to oust them.

The English dealt a great blow to the French at the battle of Sluys in 1340. An entry in Thomas de Ferrers' accounts record that the island of Guernsey, but not Castle Cornet, was back in English hands. In 1345 a force of 5 knights and 24 men-at-arms was sent from England, led by Godfrey d'Harcourt, to again try to retake the castle. Guernsey forces under de Ferrers kept watch to prevent supplies from reaching the castle by water. They also made scaling-ladders to assist in their assault on the walls. The castle was taken on or about the 16th August 1345. It was later handed back to Thomas de Ferrers, as Warden of the Isles.

The castle suffered great damage during this time and substantial rebuilding took place as a result. Written evidence from 1435 tells of the first tower built to take cannon. Situated at the north-west extremity of the castle, with a clear view over the inner roadstead and the approach to the castle, the tower is today known as the Gunners' Tower. It was later joined by a curtain wall to the Mewtis Bulwark.

The medieval castle had served the island well in a defensive role, and also provided a residence for the Warden of the Isles. The prosperity of Guernsey was greatly aided by the 1481 Papal Bull of Neutrality which gave it a new freedom to trade on both sides of the Channel during the French wars.

By the end of the medieval period many changes had taken place at the castle. A donjon or keep was built around the area of the gatehouse, which had been badly damaged, and a barbican with machicolations (see image) was raised.

Walls were strengthened as the castle grew in stature. The greatest changes, however, were a response to the challenge of new developments in weaponry.

GUERNSEY HISTORY
TIMELINE

1244–1500

1244

Other castles were built around the coast of Guernsey including one at Chateau de Marais

1294

25% of the population of St Peter Port is killed in one of the many attacks by the French

6

**WEAPONS:** THE MANGONEL

USED TO CATAPULT
ROCKS AT THE ENEMY
c1200 - 1300

*The barbican under attack.*
*A projecting gallery supported with rows of corbeled arches,*
*known as machicolations, allowed stones and boiling liquids to*
*be dropped on attackers.*

## 1338
French attack
and occupy
Guernsey

## 1394
Ste Apolline's
Chapel built

## 1400s
Guernsey fishing
trade expands into
Newfoundland
catching & salting
cod

# The Tudor Castle
## building the walls

With English involvement in Europe throughout the 1500s, the Channel Islands continued to be under the threat of invasion. Warfare had changed with the development of gunpowder and artillery, so new defences were required.

From about 1538, Henry VIII carried out a comprehensive reconstruction of his frontier defences. The Channel Islands were included and there were two main phases of reconstruction; the first between 1545 and 1558 and the second during the reign of Elizabeth I (1558 - 1603). The Governor responsible for the initial work was Sir Peter Mewtis. He paid John Rogers, a renowned master mason, the considerable sum of £40 in 1550 for his services. A bulwark to the north-west of the Gunners' Tower was constructed. Later known as the Mewtis Bulwark, it gave added protection from attack by sea or from the town, should it fall into enemy hands. In 1558, the Governor, Sir Leonard Chamberlain, wrote that *'the hole Castell of Guernsey having a very stronge and commodyus scyte, ys for the more parte ruynous and weake.'*

The Citadel was widened and platforms provided for cannon. Later known as Chamberlain's Mount, it added further protection against land-based guns. A series of Commissions recommended that the walls should be strengthened. The donjon or keep also had a platform added on the top to take cannon.

*Tudor 'Falcon' Cannon* 1
*model of the castle, circa 1570* 2
*model of Sir Thomas Leighton* 3

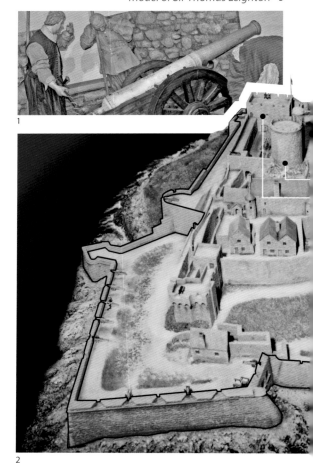

1

2

1500s — Most people still spoke Norman-French

1556 — Protestant Cauches women are burnt at the stake in St Peter Port

# Sir Thomas Leighton
## Guernsey Governor

Sir Thomas Leighton succeeded Chamberlain as Governor in 1570, remaining in post until 1610. Many of the changes to Castle Cornet under his governorship were the responsibility of Paul Ivy, the foremost military engineer of his day. Immediately after he arrived in Guernsey in 1570, Sir Thomas reported that the fortifications of the castle were in poor order;

*'… the ancient building is but stone and clay without mortar, and at every low tide, men may come a hundred abreast dry shod, from the town to the castle.'*

He complained that Chamberlain's work was unfinished and the provision for ordnance and gunpowder was inadequate. Throughout his long governorship, Leighton executed the Queen's duties with great vigour and was not always popular. It appears from surviving documents that he was often in dispute with the Guernsey authorities.

The survival of the 'Declared accounts' for the period tell us that in 1574, £300 was spent on the outer defences of the castle including the Great Gate. Other works at this time included repairs to the Tour Carré, the Turnpike by the Barbican and the Victualler's Hall.

The second phase was carried out under Paul Ivy who built new defensive walls around the medieval castle, bulwarks and bastions. These were specifically designed to protect the castle from new developments in armaments.

CHAMBERLAIN'S MOUNT

DONJON OR KEEP

TOUR CARRÉ

MEWTIS BULWARK

GREAT GATE

FROM 1570 NEW OUTER WALLS WERE BUILT
SHOWN IN RED

3

# The English Civil War
## a divided island

At the outbreak of the English Civil War in 1642, Guernsey declared its support for the cause of Parliament. Castle Cornet under its Governor, Sir Peter Osborne, remained Royalist.

Sir Peter Osborne (1584-1653) became Lieutenant Governor of Guernsey in 1621. He arrived in Guernsey in 1627 with a force of 200 men and attempted to enforce Martial Law.  In 1629 he had reinforcements sent in, for which the Island had to pay, making him very unpopular.

When Guernsey declared for Parliament in 1642, Osborne held Castle Cornet for the King.

### The Royalist Cause

The King's cause in Guernsey was supported by those who had a vested interest in the 'Establishment'- landowners and those faithful to the Church of England. A few islanders felt that the King's authority was threatened by Parliament and that the symbol of his authority, the Governor, still had validity. In Jersey the all-powerful Carteret family had provided the incumbent governor and was able to sway support for the King. In Guernsey no-one had this power, not even the Saumarez family, and the Royalists remained largely a silent minority throughout the Civil War.

### The Parliamentarian Cause

Islanders had long felt alienated from the causes of King and Country as represented by the Governor. Guernsey had lost valuable trade with Europe due to English wars. Furthermore, the Island was strong in Presbyterian and Calvinist sympathisers, whose interests were best represented by Parliament. Peter de Beauvoir, Peter Carey, and James de Havilland were the most powerful and they became Parliamentary Commissioners in 1643 after the outbreak of hostilities.

*Gun crew fires on St Peter Port* 1
*Tight stairways made the castle difficult to attack* 2
*Supplies to the castle were delivered by boat* 3

GUERNSEY HISTORY
TIMELINE
1600-1643

1642
The English Civil War begins

1642
The Island declares for Parliament but Castle Cornet remains a Royalist stronghold

10

# The Nine Year Siege
## a castle under siege

Early in 1643 the Parliamentary Commissioners for Guernsey ordered the Island authorities to apprehend the Lieutenant Governor, Sir Peter Osborne, seize all fortresses and hold the Bailiwick for Parliament. Osborne retired to Castle Cornet, his official residence and with a handful of troops (probably about 60), prepared to hold the castle. He withstood a siege for three years, sinking much of his own wealth into purchasing supplies from Jersey, England and France. During a half-hearted attack on the castle on Thursday 29 February 1643, at least six English soldiers and one Guernseyman were killed. In retaliation Osborne threatened to bombard St Peter Port. He fired a few guns and many residents evacuated the town. Parliament, wanting the castle intact, held back from bombarding it, preferring to starve out the garrison by cutting off supplies.

By the end of 1643 the support of the people of Guernsey for Parliament was wavering. This was due to a lack of protection for trading vessels and a Royalist plot to capture the new Lieutenant Governor of Guernsey, Colonel Russell, and the three Parliamentary Commissioners for Guernsey, Jurats Peter de Beauvoir, Peter Carey and James de Havilland.

1  2

3

1642
Castle Cornet holds out as a Royalist stronghold for nine years

1643
During a half-hearted attack on the castle at least six English soldiers and one Guernseyman were killed

1643
In retaliation Osborne threatens to bombard St Peter Port

11

# The Escape of the Jurats
## knife and rope

The three Commissioners were enticed aboard a ship, the 'George' of Dover, by Captain Bowden who claimed he had urgent matters from England to discuss. Once aboard, the three were received by Royalist naval officers who threatened punishment if they did not co-operate.

Sir Peter Osborne demanded that the prisoners be handed over to him as hostages. Bowden refused, having been promised a bribe by the Commissioners to land them in England.

Osborne sent a force of men to remove the prisoners into Castle Cornet, where they were lodged in a deep dungeon used to store wet musket match. The next day, they were moved into a room above, with a small window.

On 23rd November, the prisoners began cutting a hole through the floor with their knives to get at the match. A week later they had it, and were able to fashion three ropes - one to lower themselves down from the dungeon window; a second to drop them down an inner wall; and the third to get them over the outer wall onto the rocks below.

On Sunday 3rd December, with a spring tide leaving the causeway to the Town dry, and after being imprisoned for forty-three days,

the Commissioners made their escape. They were detected on the causeway and shot at, but several misfires allowed them time to get away. The three appeared in St Peter Port as the congregation was leaving church, and the news of their escape was quickly broadcast.

Osborne, it seems, had just received a Royal writ ordering their execution!

GUERNSEY HISTORY
TIMELINE
1643-1651

1643
Three commissioners were enticed aboard a ship by Captain Bowden and held captive

1643
Forty-three days after capture the three prisoners escape

1644
Peter Osborne regularly summoned to yield both the Castle and himself

12

# Besieged
## a castle under siege

By 1644 the siege had a routine. Osborne would be regularly summoned to yield both the castle and himself. He would refuse. Every few months Osborne would contact Colonel Carteret, the Governor of Jersey, and the English Royalists to plan the taking of Guernsey. The inhabitants would become alarmed and warships would be sent for. The ships would stand off for a while then go away. If the Royalists sent supply vessels they would be fired on as they unloaded. The castle would reply by firing on the Town. No serious attempt was ever made to take the castle, and two mismanaged attacks by the Parliamentarians were easily repulsed. Some damage was, however, inflicted on the castle walls by gunfire from town. St Peter Port, in return, suffered heavily from the castle's guns.

In 1644 Osborne became Governor, but in 1646 he was replaced and with the Royalist cause in England in disarray, Osborne found his way to the Continent where he died in 1653. What was left of his estate after the expenses of the siege was sequestered by Parliament.

Peter Osborne was replaced by Sir Baldwin Wake in May 1646. Wake gave up the cause in despair in May 1649 and absented himself

*The three Jurats make their escape*

without leave. He was replaced in October 1649 by Colonel Roger Burgess from Jersey.

In March 1651 an attack by the Militia on Castle Cornet was beaten off, with over thirty of the attacking force killed.

With Charles II's defeat at Worcester in Autumn 1651 the Royalist cause on the mainland foundered. One by one the Royalist garrisons, including Jersey, surrendered until only Castle Cornet held out. With command of the sea held by the Parliamentarian Navy, supplies to the castle were cut off. Finally on 19th December 1651 the little band of defenders, now only about 50 strong, was allowed to march out having received extremely favourable terms for the surrender of the castle.

**WEAPONS: CANNON**

THE MAIN WEAPON USED TO DEFEND THE CASTLE since c 1500

**1646**
The Royalist cause in England is in disarray, Osborne finds his way to the Continent where he dies

**1651**
The English Civil War comes to an end

**1651**
On 19th December the garrison surrender the castle

13

# Sir John Lambert
## & his garden

Sir John Lambert, 1619-1684, was Castle Cornet's most famous prisoner. Born at Calton, near Malham, Yorkshire, he studied Law. He married Frances Lister on 10th September 1639 and they had ten children.

On the outbreak of the Civil War in 1642 Lambert enlisted for Parliament and rose to a high rank. His Army of the North was vital to the final victory at Worcester in 1651. A courageous, skilful soldier, Lambert was a generous opponent to the Royalists. Significantly he played no part in the trial and execution of King Charles I.

'Honest John' Lambert possessed an exceptional political talent. He was instrumental in setting up the Protectorate for Cromwell, gaining for himself a seat on his Council of State, as well as the Presidency of the Army Council. He probably saw himself as Cromwell's successor, but steadfastly fought all plans to make him King.

After Cromwell's death in 1658, Lambert acted as chief negotiator for the Army in the proceedings which restored Parliament. The Royalists, expecting him to proclaim himself Protector, eagerly planned to bribe him to reinstate Charles II. Lambert was relieved of his commands and appeared before the Council of State in March 1660.  Maintaining he was unable to pay the security demanded against his good behaviour he was sent to the Tower. He escaped and tried to rally support in the Midlands, but was brought a prisoner to London.

At the Restoration of the Monarchy in May 1660, Lambert escaped fairly lightly. He had taken no part in the trial of Charles I and so avoided the death penalty. In October 1661 Lambert was exiled to Guernsey but the next summer he was brought back to London to stand trial and was found guilty of high treason. King Charles II intervened to stay his execution and Lambert returned to imprisonment in Castle Cornet.

Lord Hatton, the Governor of Guernsey was instructed to give Lambert *"such liberty and indulgence within the precincts of the Island as will consist with the liberty of his person".* Lambert, now a broken man, occupied his time in painting, needlework and the cultivation of flowers. He is reputed to

> 1681 — The privilege of Neutrality ends

> 1680s — Britain & France attempt to expand their empires worldwide

> 1681 — English government offers 'Privateers' a Letter of Marque to capture enemy ships without being branded as pirates

have introduced the Guernsey Lily (Nerine Sarniensis) into the Island.

The clandestine marriage of Lambert's daughter Mary with Governor Hatton's son Charles, strained his relations with the Governor and in 1667 Lambert was removed to the island of St Nicholas in Plymouth Sound. He died, still a prisoner, in 1684.

*Sir John Lambert tends his garden* 1
*Modern day actor tells his story* 2

| 1680s | 1680s | 1680s |
|---|---|---|
| Some Islanders generate great wealth from the capture of French ships | Increase in smuggling or 'Free trade', as the islanders called it | Quantities of wine & brandy stored in local vaults spawned a secondary industry of cask making |

# The Hatton Family
## a Guernsey Governor

The Hatton family rose to prominence when Elizabeth I appointed Christopher Hatton as Lord Chancellor. His nephew the first Lord Hatton, granted the Governorship of Guernsey in 1662, had little interest in Island affairs. When he died in 1670 he left the Government of the Island to his son Christopher, the second Lord Hatton.

Christopher held military office in Guernsey and though initially accorded scant welcome, he quickly gained the respect of the Islanders. By June 1670 he had added new buildings to the castle and taken up residence there with his mother the Lady Dowager, two of his sisters, his young wife Cecilia and their children Anne and Margaret. Only his brother Charles who had married General Lambert's daughter, and his sister Margaret were absent.

In December 1672, the family was involved in a terrible tragedy when lightning struck the castle tower igniting the powder magazine beneath. Seven people were killed and Sir Christopher moved out of the castle to take up residence in St. Peter Port. He remained there, gaining a reputation as a fair and politically adroit administrator until 1684.

1685 to 1697 were troubled years as Guernsey lost its privilege of free trade during the wars of this period. Smuggling was rife and there was constant aggravation between the Islanders and the poorly funded English garrison in the castle. Lord Hatton remained Governor until his death in 1706 - a steadying influence who served the Island well.

## GUERNSEY HISTORY
## TIMELINE

1700-1740

| 1700s | 1720s | 1700s |
|---|---|---|
| British Government imposes taxes on luxury goods imported into Britain | Guernsey becomes an entrepôt – goods were imported & stored without payment of English taxes | Guernsey becomes notorious as supply base for English, Welsh, Scottish and Irish smugglers |

# The Great Explosion
## destruction

In 1672 a powder magazine in the old keep exploded during a thunderstorm. The explosion killed seven people including the wife and mother of the Governor, Lord Hatton, and completely altered the appearance of the upper part of the castle, destroying the keep, chapel and Governor's residence. From that time, no Governor has lived in Castle Cornet.

Contemporary accounts give a graphic description of the events at the castle when just before midnight on December 29th 1672, a bolt of lightning struck the donjon or Keep, igniting the gunpowder magazine beneath it. In minutes the donjon and the buildings surrounding it were reduced to rubble.

Sir Christopher Hatton was blown onto an outer wall still alive and in his bed. His two sisters, several soldiers and a prisoner and his family also survived their injuries.

Hatton's mother the Lady Dowager, his steward William Prole and Ensign Covert were crushed to death by falling debris. Hatton's young wife Cecilia, who had run into the nursery to pray was also killed, along with her serving woman, a young girl, and the dry nurse Mistress Willis. The latter had Lord Hatton's daughter Anne in her arms and her hand on baby Margaret's cradle. Miraculously the two children escaped unhurt.

The Guernsey Court ordered a day of fasting and it was forbidden to buy anything cleared from the debris. Thirty men were sent daily to clear the site and the deaths were registered in the Town Church. The bodies of the Dowager Lady Elizabeth Hatton, and Lady Cecilia Hatton were embalmed and sent to Westminster to be buried in the tomb of the first Lord Hatton.

## 1700s

ine, rum & tobacco uggled aboard fast ps to quiet landing places in England

## 1700s

Profits from the privateering & smuggling trade are used to build fine merchants houses & invested in ships for trade

## 1740s

Methodism developed by Wesley Brothers

# Stuart Fortress
## maintaining the castle

After the Restoration of the Monarchy in 1660, Castle Cornet was fully maintained as a fortress, even though it was by now within range of cannon on Guernsey. In 1680 all Channel Island castles were put under the direction of the Board of Ordnance and the Governors were exempted from paying for their garrisons. The old Governor's Guard was soon replaced by troops of the newly established standing army.

### The Legge Report

Colonel George Legge, Lieutenant General of the Ordnance, was sent over by Royal Command to survey the defences of the Islands and make recommendations for their future security. The illustrations in the Legge Report were by Thomas Phillips, Military Engineer and later Second Engineer to James II.

The report includes costings for repairs and improvements to Castle Cornet by the celebrated Military Engineer, Bernard de Gomme which include:

*"to build a guard house next the gate £30*
*to build a small house for the gunners £30*
*to build a small house for the officers £62*
*to repair and fit up the old guard house £32"*

It appears that repairs to Castle Cornet were continually delayed. Governor Hatton wrote many letters to King Charles II begging that something should be done. It was not until the 1680 Survey that any recommendations were made, and how many were put into action is debatable. Certainly new barracks and the Saluting Battery were built, but no official residence for the Governor. As late as 1773, the then Governor, Sir Jeffrey Amherst KCB, was asked by the States of Guernsey to request the King that something should be done as the 'lodgings' used meant:

*"that the Governors and Lieutenant Governors are not able to receive in a manner worthy of the Island, not only the inhabitants of the Island, but any distinguished strangers."*

reproduced with the permission of the Royal Court

*Detail of the castle taken from the Legge Report* 1
*after the great explosion*
*Painting of the castle **before** the great explosion* 2

1740s

1740

Guernsey seafarers sail and trade around the globe during the continuing trade wars

Philip Saumarez joins Anson's round the world voyage in the Centurion and helps capture a Spanish treasure ship

PAGE
**34-35**

SURVIVING STUART FEATURES ARE SHOWN ON THE MAP

**1743**

Town Hospital opens to
support the poor and
needy

**1747**

Philip Saumarez
killed in action
against the French off
Finistère aged 37

**1756**

Seven year war
begins between
France & England

# Domestic Life in the Castle
## a hard life

With the presence of the English garrison in Castle Cornet, archaeological evidence shows there were always women and children too. Women would have been involved in domestic arrangements, from those of the Lieutenant Governor when he lived here, down to those of the common soldiers.

British Army regiments, when in garrison, had a certain number of soldiers' wives with them, on the strength of the regiment. More women would follow unofficially, and liaisons with local women would inevitably take place.

The soldier's woman was more than a camp follower and provided an essential service. The lot of a soldier's woman in the 18th and 19th centuries was a hard one. In barracks, privacy was non-existent, and she could find herself washing and catering for an entire company of men though despised by officers as immoral and as a thief.

The records of the Town Hospital in St Peter Port are a harrowing testimony to the harshness of their lives - abandoned and abused women and infants, disease and mental disorder are common entries, and must have represented a severe strain on the resources of the Island.

The Upper Barracks (now the Maritime Museum) built in 1745, were adapted for use as Married Quarters during the late 1870s. These were used up until 1939 when the last garrison regiment marched out. There are still people who can remember playing as children in and around the walls and guns of the Castle.

*Soldiers at rest in the Lower Barracks* 1
*The wife of a soldier prepares a meal* 2

GUERNSEY HISTORY
TIMELINE

1776-1799

1776
American Declaration of Independence

1776
James Saumarez proves his gallantry with a fierce attack on Fort Sullivan

20

1   2

## 1780
Fort George is built to replace Castle Cornet as a garrison fort

## 1787
The Duke of Richmond commissions a survey of the Island

## 1794
James Saumarez thwarts a French attempt to invade Guernsey

21

# The Napoleonic Wars
## increased tension

After the 1672 explosion, Castle Cornet was repaired, although the keep was not rebuilt. It was no longer ideal for first-line defence, it was cramped and access was difficult. Worst of all it was overlooked by the high ground above St Peter Port and well in range of artillery placed there. However, with increased international tension in the mid 1700s leading to the Napoleonic Wars it was still an important fortress, armed with over 70 guns and with a garrison of up to 300 men.

### The Bombproof Barracks

The building of the Upper Barracks in 1745 was followed by barrack quarters constructed between 1786 and 1790, consisting of two bombproof casemates to house 195 men under the Citadel. These were built in the 'Hollow Ground' and filled over, linking with the surviving vaults of the old Tour Carré. Positions for guns were located above them. Invalid companies moved into the new barracks in November 1790. By 1830 they were unoccupied because of damp. In 1901 they were adapted for storage of ammunition to serve the new 12-pounder Quick Firing guns installed on the Castle Citadel above. A report of 1847 recommended the sacrificing of existing buildings in the castle and their replacement by further bombproofs -

*"The position is by nature so strong that by obtaining flanked escarps that could not be silenced or breached from a distance, a small garrison thoroughly protected with all its necessary Stores, ammunition etc by ample Bomb proofs, ought to hold out in it almost for ever.*

*To gain this end it would be expedient to sacrifice any existing building or construction that impeded that end .........."*

Building the Upper Barracks   1
Castle Cornet at low tide by Peter Le Lievre   2
Castle Cornet circa 1785   3

GUERNSEY HISTORY
TIMELINE

1799–1815

1799

Napoleon Bonaparte is ruler of France and much of Europe

1803

Sir John Doyle instigates ambitious programme of reclamation and rebuilding as part of defensive strategy

reproduced with the permission of the Royal

22

2

3

1804

The Braye du Valle
is drained and
Guernsey becomes
one island

1812

Guernseyman
Major General Isaac Brock
is instrumental in saving
Upper Canada for Britain

1800s

Country people still speak
Norman - French and are
largely involved in agriculture,
fishing and quarrying

# Gun Platform
## artillery in the castle

### Gun Platform

In 1812 the British Garrison moved its headquarters to the newly-constructed Fort George. The castle's role changed to serving as a gun platform for the defence of the east coast and St Peter Port. Heavier guns were brought in and the upper part of the castle changed to accommodate new fortifications technology.

### Artillery in the Castle

The various reports on Castle Cornet written for the Board of Ordnance and the War Department after 1855 provide a picture of general neglect, with periodic flurries of repair and improvement. Armament was often left unmounted and until about 1870 comprised muzzle loaders of various calibres. Traversing platforms for most of the fixed guns were eventually built and in the early 1870s the technology was uprated by the provision of six 7inch Armstrong Rifled Muzzle Loading Guns (110-pounder) on the Cavalier battery. These provided the major armament until 1901 when they were replaced by two 12-pounder Quick Firing guns.

The main or 'Grand' Magazine of the castle was situated in the Lower Ward close to the Lower Barracks, and surrounded by a blast wall. It was replaced by an underground magazine higher in the castle in about 1870, and a new Guard Room (now the castle shop) was built in its place.

### The Royal Garrison Artillery

The Royal Garrison Artillery manned the fixed coastal defences of Great Britain and the Empire.

Until the early 20th century and standardisation, there was an enormous variety of guns, old and new, in coastal defences. These required the manufacture of a vast range of ammunition and the complicated training of men in the mounting and handling of all the different kinds of guns.

The Lower Barracks continued to be used to house men of the Royal Garrison Artillery until the end of the 1914-18 War. Between the wars the castle was home to a detachment of the Island's garrison infantry regiment, and its band usually occupied the Lower Barracks. Some improvement to facilities were made such as gas lighting in about 1880, but basically the accommodation remained unaltered for many years.

1816-1845

First local currency minted to finance the building of the markets

Cholera epidemic, 99 people die in three weeks

The first Guernsey Tourist Guide is published

*A posed photograph of a swimmer and a local fisherman taken on the ramparts of the Saluting Battery in the 1930s. At this time the Battery still carried seven 40pdr Amstrong breechloading guns which dated from around 1864.*

# Victoria & Beyond
## a new defensive role

In the early years of the nineteenth century the open ground on the Citadel was roofed over to provide bombproof barrack accommodation. On top of it the 'Cavalier' Battery housed heavy guns. An underground magazine was later added to the castle. In 1860 the castle was physically connected to Guernsey by a breakwater, built as part of the harbour reconstruction.

### Harbour Defence

When a Defence Plan for Guernsey was drawn up in 1904, France was still perceived to be the potential enemy. In the event however, France was an ally when war was declared on Germany in 1914. Castle Cornet's primary role, along with other batteries, was to protect the harbour and shipping from surface or submarine attack.

### The Great War 1914 -18

On the outbreak of war in 1914, a previously devised plan was put into operation. Although Fort George remained the HQ for the garrison, manning of Castle Cornet was augmented. The married quarters were cleared of wives and children for the increased number of men. The wartime garrison stood at 80 men of the Royal Garrison Artillery, with daily reliefs from the Royal Guernsey Militia Artillery, and 17 regular infantrymen detached from Fort George.

1

1846
Queen Victoria made the first Royal visit to the island

1846
French writer Victor Hugo settles in Guernsey

1848
Victoria Tower commemorating the Queen's visit is built

PAGE
**34-35**

THE CITADEL & CAVALIER BATTERY ARE SHOWN ON THE MAP

2

4

3

*The bridge to the castle under construction* 1
*Ladies and gentlemen pose alongside cannons inside the castle* 2 & 3
*A stroll along the new castle connecting 'bridge'* 4

**1905**
First football
Muratti match
between
Guernsey &
Jersey

**1914-18**
Many Guernseymen
lose their lives as part
of the Royal Guernsey
Light Infantry fighting
in France

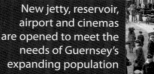

**1928-39**
New jetty, reservoir,
airport and cinemas
are opened to meet the
needs of Guernsey's
expanding population

# The Occupation 1940-1945
## Hafenschloss

The last Garrison Regiment was stationed in Guernsey in 1939. With the fall of France in 1940 the Channel Islands were considered undefendable and were left to be occupied by the Germans. The Islands were seen by the occupying force as a part of the Atlantic Wall, and massive concrete emplacements for guns and equipment were built. In Castle Cornet these were built on top of earlier works, to uprate it for its role as part of the harbour and anti-aircraft defences. Castle Cornet is probably the only British castle to have been strafed by the RAF!

Castle Cornet formed part of the air defence cover of the harbour and town of St Peter Port. The castle was armed with two 3.7cm Flak (Anti-Aircraft) guns and three 2cm guns which were in action many times, particularly when air raids were carried out on shipping and harbour installations in St Peter Port.

### Hafenschloss

To the occupying Germans, Castle Cornet was known as Hafenschloss (Harbour Castle). The castle was garrisoned by men of a Luftwaffe Flak (Anti-Aircraft) unit comprising 1 officer (commanding the castle), 14 NCOs and 36 men. These were augmented by detachments from the Navy and Army. At times there were 300 men in the castle.

Concrete emplacements and bunkers in the castle housed Anti-Aircraft guns, machine guns and grenade throwers, whilst the rock outside the castle had defensive roll-bombs. In the event of an attack from the Town, the castle bridge would have been blown up with built in demolition charges, isolating the castle as it had been in previous centuries. An Anti-Submarine boom and net, closing off the harbour entrance, ran between Castle Cornet and the White Rock.

1   *Barbed wire defences around the castle*
2   *German anti-aircraft gun crew*
3   *Some German structures within the castle are marked with female names*

image courtesy: the Priaulx Library

GUERNSEY HISTORY
TIMELINE

1940–1945

| 1939 | 1940 | 1940 |
| --- | --- | --- |
| Great Britain declares war on Germany | Many islanders leave for the UK abandoning their homes and businesses | Guernsey is occupied by German Forces |

28

PAGE
**34-35**
GERMAN CONCRETE FORTIFICATIONS ARE SHOWN ON THE MAP

2

1

3

## WEAPONS: 2 CM FLAK 38

The 2cm Flak 38 was introduced in 1938 as a standard light anti-aircraft gun for the Wehrmacht and as such it was used by Army, Waffen-SS and Luftwaffe units. Its normal detachment was six men and it could, if required be broken down into six units for them to carry. Barrel recoil and residual gas pressure operated its automatic breech and firing action, and its rate of fire was 220 to 450 rounds per minute. Maximum vertical range was 4012 yards. Ammunition came in High Explosive or Armour Piercing forms and was loaded in 20-round magazines.

**1942**
Islanders born in Great Britain are sent to internment camps in Germany

**1944**
The local population is saved from starvation by the Red Cross

**1945**
Guernsey is liberated by British forces on the 9th May

# The Castle Today
## welcomes visitors

After the Second World War the castle was handed back to the Island. Today it has become the Island's premier tourist attraction housing a selection of museums and home to a number of special events.

Above all, it stands proudly as a symbol of Guernsey's military heritage and significance. It is representative of the determination of islanders to defend their independence.

For all the latest news about the castle and our museums please visit our website at:
**www.museums.gov.gg**

© Chris Andrews

image courtesy visitguernsey

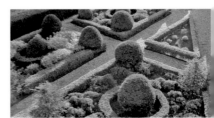

GUERNSEY HISTORY
# TIMELINE

| 1946 | 1950-70 | 1950-70 |
|---|---|---|
| 1946-TODAY | The beginning of a period of peace and prosperity for the island | The island's economy relies largely on horticulture and tourism | The tomato export becomes well known as the Guernsey Tom and greenhouse building booms |

© Chris Andrews

© Chris Andrews

© Chris Andrews

# The Castle Today
## museums

Within the castle walls some of the buildings have been adapted to house museums, a café, shop and visitor facilities.

Our museums tell the story of the castle and the people who built and served within it; the affiliated 201 RAF Squadron; Guernsey's maritime heritage; the Royal Guernsey Militia and Royal Guernsey Light Infantry.

Please be advised that a rolling programme of refurbishment and installation of new displays may mean that certain galleries are temporarily closed.

PAGE
**34-35**  CASTLE BUILDINGS ARE SHOWN ON THE MAP

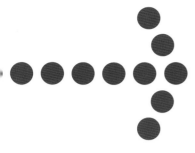

3

5

4

6

© British Crown Copyright/MOD

1 *The Story of Castle Cornet Museum*
2 *Quayside reconstruction, Maritime Museum*
3 *Royal Guernsey Light Infantry*
4 *Salting conger, Maritime Museum*
5 *U-Boat attack, 201 Squadron RAF Museum*
6 *Nimrod aircraft, 201 Squadron RAF Museum*

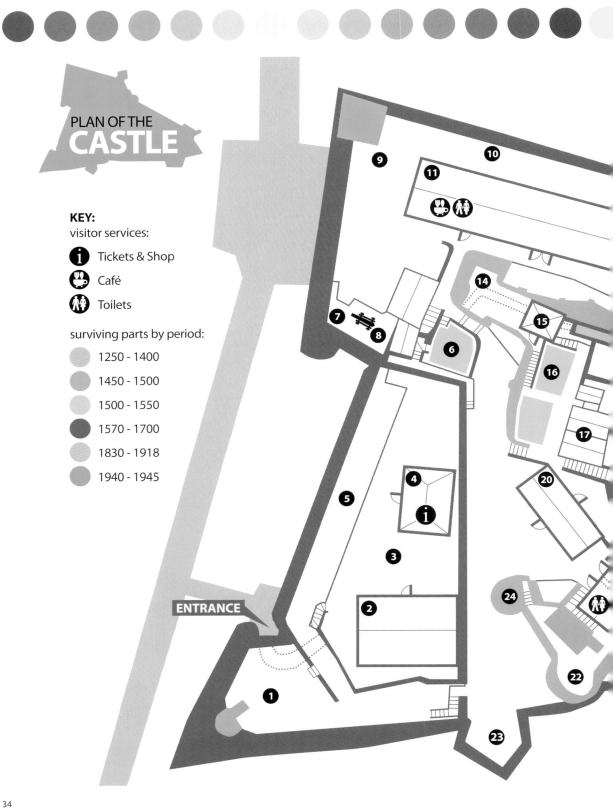

## PLAN OF THE CASTLE

**KEY:**

visitor services:

- Tickets & Shop
- Café
- Toilets

surviving parts by period:

- 1250 - 1400
- 1450 - 1500
- 1500 - 1550
- 1570 - 1700
- 1830 - 1918
- 1940 - 1945

ENTRANCE